CAPTURE MINNESOTA II™

Minnesota Through the Eyes of Minnesota Photographers

Presented by

SAINT PAUL | MINNEAPOLIS

Foreword

You've just opened an amazing book of photography.

The fact that it comes from a wide variety of photographers in an eclectic mix of locations around Minnesota makes it even more impressive.

Now in our second year, *tpt*'s Capture Minnesota project is going strong. We created new, thoughtful challenges; attracted submissions from hundreds of photographers new to the Capture community; and we ended up with over 125,000 new photos from both new and established participants.

Whether you just picked up this book out of curiosity, took a photo that ended up inside or were a key voter who shaped the beauty on the following pages, you're holding a representation of the best new photography in Minnesota.

So have a seat, and start leafing through it. We hope you enjoy it.

Thank you!

Want to know more about this project from *tpt*, or upload your own work? Please visit us at www.captureminnesota.com

Table of Contents

About This Book

Capture Minnesota™ is a unique approach to fine-art book publishing. An online community of local photographers submitted photos to be considered for this book. Then, area residents voted to determine which photos would be published. From 222,705 photo submissions to the pages of this book, 8,786,491 votes helped shape what you hold in your hands. It's Minnesota through the eyes and lenses of local photographers and enthusiasts. Enjoy!

Join the Community

Every bit of this book was made possible by an active community of users on the Capture Minnesota Web site. Whether you're a professional photographer, hobbyist, or just like looking at great Minnesota photography, join the community at Capture Minnesota (captureminnesota.com).

How to Use This Book

Open. Look at the best photography you've ever seen. Repeat. Actually, maybe there's a little more to it. First, be sure to note the credit listed with each photo. Search for your favorite photographer at Capture Minnesota (captureminnesota.com) and leave your comment or show your appreciation with a vote. Many photographers also sell their photos online so you may be able to buy a print for your wall! Also note, captions are used as submitted by the photographer, mostly verbatim. We do our best to fact check, but captions may not be perfect.

Copyright Details

LANDMARKS AND ARCHITECTURE

Landmarks and architectural details from cities and rural areas.

RASPBERRY ISLAND BANDSHELL BY DAVID DEAN (above): Downtown St. Paul along with the artfully designed bandshell.

MINNESOTA HISTORY CENTER BY ANDY BELL (left): I went to St. Paul earlier in the week with Peter Wong hoping to capture the full moon rising over the St. Paul skyline. Instead, I found this.

-5 DEGREES BY MARK NICHOLSON (far left): It may be cold outside, but not in here.

PILLSBURY BY TJ LARSON (above): Historic Building A.

COMO CONSERVATORY BY ERIK BJORUM (left): Great architectural landmark.

WALKER HENNEPIN NIGHT BY NORBERT MARKLIN (opposite): Dusk on Hennepin Avenue.

UNIVERSITY OF MINNESOTA BY RICHARD DAVID (below): Took this shot today when I took my dad to Fairview for his check.

GUTHRIE AT SUNSET BY GRETA LARSON (above): I recently went to Minneapolis and the yellow floor in the Guthrie Theater. No one was there, so some of my friends and I just lay around on the benches and took a few cool pictures. This is such a lovely room and every time I'm up there I wish that I could make it my bedroom.

WINDOWS BY DAVID RALPH JOHNSON (right): Warehouse District, Minneapolis.

OPPOSITE:

STONE ARCH AT SUNRISE BY PAMELA MANDEVILLE (1): Yes, I got up early! Actually, I happened to look out my window and saw the beautiful colors of the sunrise. I took a drive downtown which is fortunately not far because the sky changes so quickly! This is, of course, the Stone Arch Bridge with the Carlyle Condos in the background.

THROUGH THE RED WINDOW BY REYMAN DE LOS SANTOS (2): Taken from a farm in Grant.

THE DESTINATION BY KAREN HUNNICUTT-MEYER (3): "All of life is a journey which paths we take, what we look back on, and what we look forward to is up to us. We determine our destination, what kind of road we will take to get there, and how happy we are when we get there." - unknown

AUTUMN REFLECTION BY JOAN M ROOD (4): Taken while visiting Grand Portage.

DOORS BY SHAWN BROWN (5): "There are things known, and things unknown, and in between there are doors." - Jim Morrison

GLENSHEEN STAINED GLASS BY PATTI TOLO (6): The stained glass centerpiece at the Glensheen Historic Estate, pictured here, stands almost 12 feet tall and overlooks the terrace, gardens and Lake Superior. The window is on the second level of the grand staircase and hand-made by European artisans over 100 years ago.

BARN WINDOW BY KATE TAYLOR (7): A red Minnesota barn.

NEGLECTED BY KATE THOMAS (8): I love to shoot old windows and this certainly caught my eye.

ROOM WITH A VIEW BY RAY KLEMPKA (9): The window of a one-room schoolhouse. The lines reminded me of ruled notebook paper.

ALONE BY JAYME LARSON (above): An old man sits alone on the steps of St. Mary's Cathedral.

SUPPORT YOUR PIERS BY BOB PETERSON (left): These are piers supporting the spans of the I-494 bridge over the Minnesota River and its floodplain. This is actually two bridges; one for eastbound traffic and one for westbound traffic. Note the curve of the bridge. My camera was pointed west.

WARPED AROUND FOG BY MICHAEL BENHAM (far left): During a heavy foggy day in early December, I headed downtown in the early afternoon to take advantage of the photo opportunities. This is a straight up fisheye shot outside the IDS Center on 8th St.

THE ROAD TO NOWHERE BY JUSTIN PRUDEN (above): A foggy morning envelops the Stillwater Bridge.

DULUTH LIFT BRIDGE BY DAVID PARKER (right): While up in Duluth this past weekend, I had some time to wander around Canal Park.

BRIDGE BY SEAMLESS MEDIA (opposite): Lowry Avenue Bridge.

LATTICE OF LIGHT
BY MIKE PLUCKER (top): In this image is St. Paul's Raspberry Island's Schubert Club Bandshell. Architect and designer James Carpenter designed the structure using stainless steel lattice and offset pipes and rod diagonals. The laminated glass that covers the structure creates an ethereal look when lit up at night. The bandshell was completed in September 2002. I used a 30-second exposure to allow the lights from St. Paul to fully illuminate the bandshell.

REFLECTION | NOITCELFER
BY JEREMY JORDAN (far left): The reflection on the Mississippi River tonight was stunning, the water was clear and moving really slowly, plus the cold temps helped clear the air.

FOGGY NIGHT
BY WERNER ROLAND (bottom left): Foggy night in downtown Minneapolis.

STONE ARCH BRIDGE
BY JENNIFER J FRISMANIS (bottom right): The beautifully lit Stone Arch Bridge, and the tail lights of my ride home driving away....

CATHEDRAL AT DUSK
BY JAMES JERSKEY (following left top): This landmark has punctuated each and every sunset for the past 100 years. I captured this from the steps of the State Capitol.

JUST ADD METALLIC SALTS
BY RON TRAEGER (following left bottom): This is part of the stained glass panels on the St. John's University Church.

LET THE SUN SHINE
BY JOHN LOMBARDI (following middle): The sun shining in the St. Paul Cathedral dome.

INTERIOR - ST. PAUL CHURCH
BY ALEXANDRA PETROVA (following right): Amazing details of the St. Paul Cathedral.

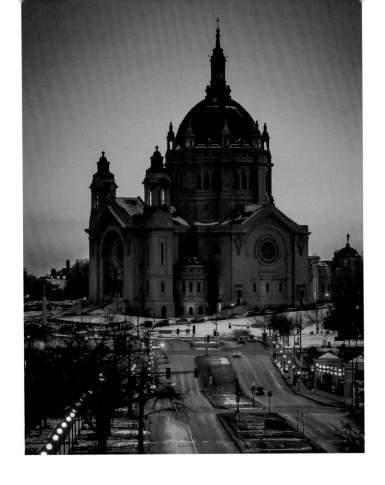

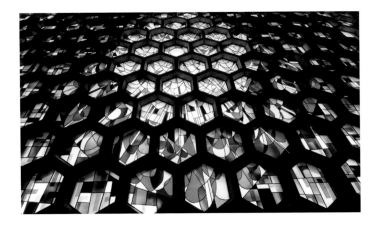

CAPITOL CIRCLE BY RACHEL CAIN (above): View in Minnesota State Capitol.

CLASSIC LOBBY BY DAVE ADAMS (left): Landmark Center lobby.

MAN VS. GOD BY MEGS MOLNAU (far left): Taken at the Minneapolis City Hall. If God made man in his image, do we also create in his?

TAKE THE STAGE BY TOMMY SAR (opposite): View of the auditorium from the stage at the Orpheum Theatre.

STONE ARCH BRIDGE BY BRYAN KING (above): Panorama of the Stone Arch Bridge at night.

ICED UP BY TONI KAHNKE (left): This is located at the picnic area at Gooseberry Falls.

CRISSCROSSING STAIRS BY DAVE ADAMS (opposite left): Main stairway at the Downtown St. Paul Public Library.

LONG CLIMB BY ERIN CROWDER (opposite right): A stairway to Split Rock Lighthouse.

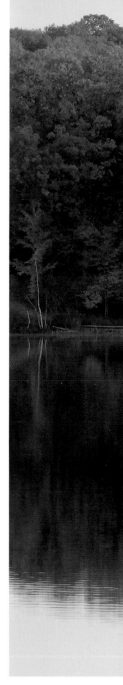

LAKE SUPERIOR ANGRY BY FUNKY SPACECAT (above): Some days the big lake just seems really angry...like she wants to kill someone... "red sky by morning, photographer take warning."

GRAND MARAIS LIGHTHOUSE AND GULLS BY PETER ELVIN (right): A flock of gulls flies near the Grand Marais lighthouse at sunrise.

AUTUMN REFLECTIONS BY ROGER DULLINGER (far right): The setting sun highlights the fall colors in the woods surrounding Stella Maris Chapel on Lake Sagatagan at Saint John's University in Collegeville.

FUN: MINNESOTA STYLE
Sports, recreation, celebrations, festivals, food and music in Minnesota.

AIRSTREAM TLC BY ERIC MUELLER (above): WWII Bomber getting some much-needed attention.

FLYING OVER THE SUN BY RUSSELL LOFGREN JR (left): Powered parasail enthusiast enjoying the setting sun over West Arm Bay, Lake Minnetonka.

THUNDER IN THE VALLEY BY MAX HAYNES (far left): Members of the T-6 Thunder North American Flight Team join forces with the Minnesota Wing of the Commemorative Air Force's B-25 "Miss Mitchell" on a glorious fall flight over the valleys and hollows along the Mississippi River.

TIGHT FORMATION BY CARL SCHULZETENBERG (above): Members of the Blue Angels fly in tight formation at an air show in St. Cloud.

UP AND AWAY BY RAY KLEMPKA (right): A young couple played copilot with one of the bigger kites at Lake Harriet. Winds picked up considerably in the afternoon. I wondered if they were going to get picked up by this flying dragon.

BELOW THE BALLOON BY DAVID PARKER (far right): Being it is summertime, the hot air balloons are launching again. This one went right over our house.

CAMPING UNDER THE STARS
BY BEN BERNDT (right): Ever since I was a young boy, camping under the stars in the north woods has been one of my absolute favorite things to do. This photo was taken on a recent trip into the Boundary Waters Canoe Area on a particularly stormy night. As I was walking back from the campfire, I noticed the sky had cleared just enough and the photo popped into my head.

FISHING AT SUNRISE
BY ELLEN LYSNE ALBERG (far right): Looking for the first catch of the day admits a foggy sunrise on Lake Sarah near Erskine. This is my husband's aunt and uncle, we were having a family camping trip. This was a beautiful morning and I was lucky enough to capture this photo. This is one of my favorites in all my years taking photos.

ROWING THROUGH THE COLORS... BY H BROWN TON (above): I was focusing on the autumn color reflections when the rowers entered my view... I had about 10 seconds to readjust to capture this shot before my line of sight was blocked.

OPPOSITE:

SO HAPPY TO CATCH ONE BY ALAN SCHULZETENBERG (1): The pure joy and pride young children share when catching that first fish is something to treasure.

Size doesn't matter. The type of fish doesn't matter. It's the excitement, fun and pleasure that make this time special!

ROW BOAT BY CHRIS MEIUM (2): The trusty row boat on Lake Florida.

CUTTING THE WALL BY FRANCO COLAIANNI (3): Slalom skier cutting a wall of water on Lake Minnetonka.

HEADING OUT BY PETER DE SIBOUR (4): Lake in the Boundary Waters.

AT THE FISHIN' HOLE BY JIM ERICSON (5): What a fine day to take a stroll and wander by the fishin' hole. I can't think of a better way to pass the time o' day. Taken at Silverwood Park in Saint Anthony Village.

THE DOCK BY SUSAN DYRUD MACDONALD (6): My children, relaxing on a dock in Wayzata.

RED WING BARN BY CASSANDRA PARKER (7): Barn, Red Wing, Minn.

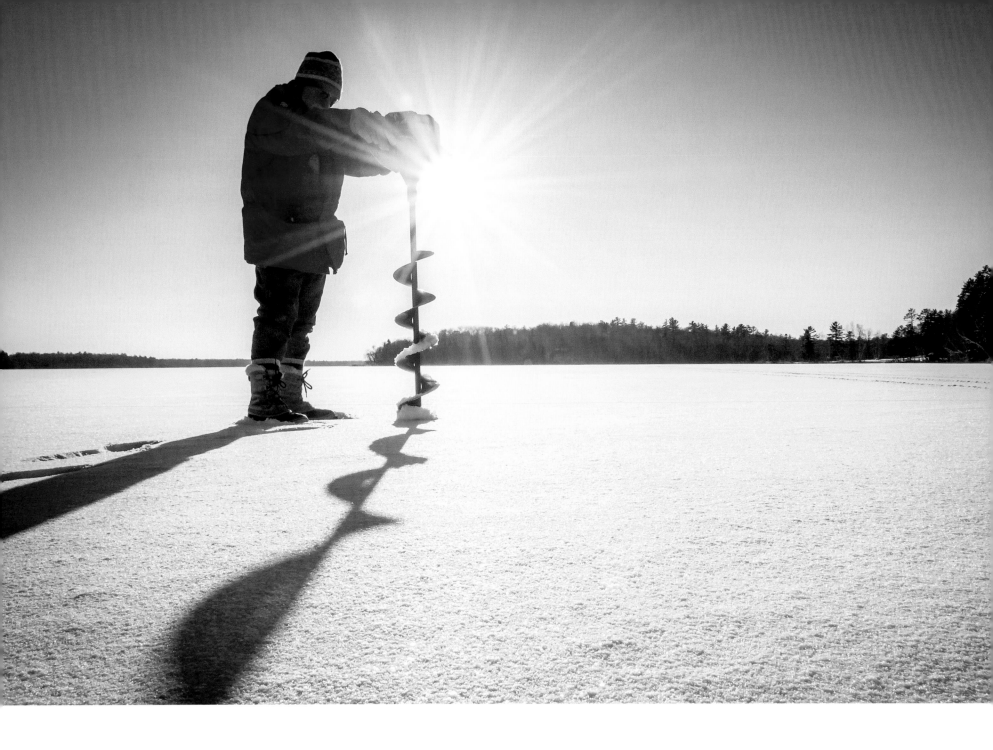

ICE BOATS ON LAKE PEPIN BY AL MUELLER (left): Ice boats being assembled on Jan. 26, 2013 for the 13th Gold Cup World DN Championship.

FIRING UP THE AUGER BY NIK ROWELL (far left): Picking an ice fishing spot on a cold winter evening.

RIVER BOAT BY JEFF BARTELT (below): Early morning finds a traditional-style paddle boat docked along Lake Pepin in southeastern Minnesota.

RUCK OVER! BY MAX HAYNES (above): A downed player for St. Cloud State's rugby team must give up the ball while a battle rages above him to gain control. Winona State players pushed with all their might, but St. Cloud won the day.

RAWLINGS BY ANNA GALL (left top): Just for fun.

GAME ON BY P.R. JOHNSON (left bottom): Are you ready for some football?

LEARNING TO FLY BY ANDY BELL (opposite): This young player from Austin prepares to take flight on his way home from third while taking on the Eagan Wildcats 10A team.

SQUEEZE IN TIGHT BY WENDELL TAGROS (following left): Minnesota Stars and Rowdies players try to squeeze in and get a better position for a headshot.

BACK LIT JOGGER BY GEORGE PETERS (following right): Jogger catching the last rays of the day after a storm passed through Lake Calhoun.

THE RACE
BY BRIAN BILLADEAU (above left):
Mudding it up at Canterbury Park on turn three.

BARREL RACE
BY ROOKY STUDIOS (above right): Fierce competition in Saint Louis County at the fairgrounds.

RODEO BLUR BY JAYME LARSON (right):
Barrel racing at the Isanti Rodeo.

I WANT TO BE A COWBOY...
BY ANDREW CHOW (opposite): Unless I have to do this!

BORN TO PULL BY CHRIS GIBBS (above): A focused lead dog at the John Beargrease start.

MINNESOTA BMX RACING BY MARK CONLEY (left): Minnesota racer Elliot McGrath.

PHOTO FINISH BY CHRIS JOHNSON (opposite): These two riders were battling the whole race.

WATCH THIS DAD!
BY MAX HAYNES (above left): Riley Haynes makes one last leap back to summer as an early snowfall turns the tides on the seasons.

ABLE TO LEAP COLD WATER
BY STEPHEN PACHOLL (above right): White Bear Lake Polar Plunge 2012.

2004 ST. PAUL WINTER CARNIVAL ICE PALACE ILLUMINATION
BY NORBERT MARKLIN (left): This is the evening view of the Ice Palace from the rooftop of the Holiday Inn across the street. Brrrrrrrrrrrrrr - it was cold up there!

ORANGE POPSICLE
BY MIKE PLUCKER (far left): Mall of America Ice Castle.

CHRISTMAS LIGHTS BY KATHY SCHROEDER (above): Winter lights.

CRYSTAL BLUE NEW YEAR BY PETER DE SIBOUR (right): Reflecting on the holidays.

IN CHRISTMAS SPIRIT BY CHRISTOPHER FRANKLIN (far right): Overlooking the Minnesota Valley Wildlife Refuge, a sparkling tree shines with the spirit of Christmas.

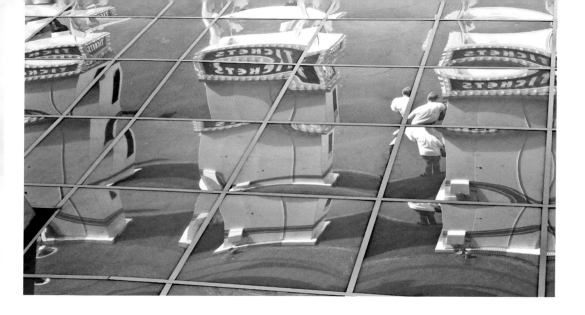

SKYWHEEL BY LANE PELOVSKY (above): Long exposure of a Midway ride at the 2011 Minnesota State Fair.

TICKETS BY JENNIFER HALBERT (left top): Minnesota State Fair reflection.

WOODEN HORSE BY KATHY SCHROEDER (left bottom): Having fun.

ORANGE BY PENNY MOUNSDON (below): Sunset at the county fair.

MARQUEE BY PAT NICHOLSON (opposite): Marquee.

FAIRY GREETER BY GINA STOCKER (above): A fairy from the Renaissance Festival.

SUNRISE SALUTE BY WALLY STADICK (right top): Every July 4th, Burg's Battery has a thirteen-gun salute at the cemetery in New Ulm at sunrise.

CAREFUL WITH THE SWORD! BY ARIEL ARIEL (right bottom): This photo was taken at the Japanese Lantern Festival in Como Park. Not my usual photography subject but I liked how the flying sheet of water was captured along with a victorious expression on his face.

RADIANT BY TOMMY SAR (above): "If your pictures aren't good enough, you're not close enough." - Robert Capa. Is this close enough? Her feathers were swiping my lens!

WAR CRY BY IVY VAINIO (left): Ben Spears, Red Lake Ojibwe member and traditional dancer, lets out a "war cry" at a powwow in Sawyer.

MUSIC STIRS THE SOUL BY JIM TESKE (below): The Landing at Minnesota River Heritage Park. "When you lose the power of wonder, you grow old, no matter how old you are. If you have the power of wonder, you are forever young. The whole world is pristine and new and exciting." - Sigurd F. Olson

BELIEVE BY MARK BERTELSON (left top): Minnesota is known for its many excellent dance schools and dedicated dancers.

ASANTE CHILDREN'S CHOIR MEMBER BY GARY HANSON (far left): It's all in the heart. The Asante Children's Choir travels throughout Minnesota.

FACE TO FACE BY STAN WALDHAUSER (opposite): Student dance performance.

SUN DANCE BY JOHN HEINO (below): Zenith City Lines: a collaborative project with the talented dancers of Duluth's Avalon Performing Arts Company.

IN THE MOOD BY DARIN LUEHRS (above): Dan and Art set the mood at Homespun on the Homestead with their wonderful singing and instrumentation on the banjo, guitar, fiddle and mandolin. Great job fellas!

IN TUNE BY JAMES GILLILAND (left): Time to tune up the guitar and take a little break for a few notes...

THE PERCUSSIONIST BY STEPHEN PACHOLL (far left): Cactus Blossoms at Lee's Liquor Lounge.

RUNDOWN ROCKSTAR BY NATE GIBSON (opposite): One picture from a series I took for a friends' guitar blog. Shot in an alley near the farmers market in Downtown St. Paul.

FIZZY STRAWBERRY
BY SUSAN FEULNER (above left): Strawberry in soda water.

WHOLE GRAIN 5 & ROASTED CORN PANCAKE WITH AVOCADO MOUSSE & BAJA SHRIMP
BY ROB YURETICH (above right): The best part of my food photo shoots is tasting the final product.

FRESH RASPBERRIES
BY RUSS STOECKEL (right): Fresh at the Farmers Market.

SUMMIT
BY JILLIAN HELLELOID (far right): A whole lotta Summit!

SEIZE THE DAY BY MELINDA MARTIN (above): Nine Nights of Music brought out dancers young and old at the Minnesota History Center. As seen, some enjoyed it more than others.

UNREAL BY NICO DE WAL (right): Chuck Close's "Frank" at the Minneapolis Institute of Arts with the silhouette of a man examining it closely. Looking at it (even) closely, you would think this is a photograph, but if that's what you think, then Chuck Close just fooled you. It's a painting.

NOSTALGIC EVENING BY GARY MICHELS (opposite): Hastings Classic Car Show.

MINNESOTA PEOPLE

Family, friends, children and other portraits of characters across Minnesota.

FRANCIS E. ROBERTSON AND APRIL. LITTLE SWAN, MINNESOTA BY BRANDON LEPASTI (above): This is a photo from my Iron Range series. My grandfather stands for a portrait with his Palomino, April.

JAKE'S JUNK BY JOHN LOMBARDI (left): A young lady looks out this old truck's window at Hot Sams.

TAKE OFF BY CAITLIN O'BRIEN (far left): This was on the photo walk I did with two other photographers. The boys laughed when I ran back and forth to my camera (since I forgot my remote).

HOMEGROWN MINNESOTA TWIN 2027 BY O. STOKES (above): This little guy of "The Train Museum" notoriety is back as a catcher in coach's pitch baseball.

DRUM BEARER BY ROBERT MEYERS (left): Carrying a large drum at a festival celebrating the remodeling of the Minneapolis Institute of Arts.

ALLEY IN WONDERLAND BY JILL HYLAND (opposite left top): Alley Hanson in the rose garden at the Minnesota Landscape Arboretum. The Minnesota Landscape Arboretum is part of the University of Minnesota and includes over 1,000 acres of beautiful scenery and gardens.

YOU SWING FROM YOUR TREE. I'LL SWING FROM MINE. BY PHYL BONER (opposite left bottom): Self portrait.

STUNNING SMILE BY MIROSLAV SKORYKH (opposite right): This senior was just amazing at the shoot. She's one of my favorites from all the seniors that I have shot.

CHILDREN'S PARADISE BY MERCY NYGAARD (above): Bubbles and The State Fair! What more could a kid ask for?

OPPOSITE:

DAYDREAM BY SHELLEY PEARSON (1): I was taking photographs of my friend's three children; when I turned from photographing two of them I found their little middle man lost in thought and was able to capture this image before he moved.

COLORFUL BY SUSAN MONTGOMERY (2): I pulled this old pic out, to literally warm my heart, even though it was physically freezin' outside today. I also needed to reflect with some memory. My daughter went back to school, so our winter break officially ended. This is one of my favorite pics of my kids one summer, by Old Arizona in south Minneapolis.

BROTHER & SISTER BY TIMOTHY GALDUNICK (3): They probably will not always get along so well. :)

BOMBER HAT KID BY WENDY EBERT (4): No worries about being cold here.

SECOND HAND RAIN BY LISA HANNIGAN (5): My grandson, Nolan, had just flicked the tree branch and the tree rained down the rain drops it had collected that morning.

GAVINO BY JUDY PARKER (6): Gets his thunderhawk.

10 PERFECT TOES BY ANDY BELL (above left): My brother took a break with his 11 day old grandson to count the many things to be thankful for at our family gathering. Congrats to my brother Ernie on becoming a grandpa and my wonderful niece on becoming a mom!

BROTHERS IN A BUCKET BY JENNIE GASKINS (above right): LOVE that they all tried to squeeze themselves into one bucket...the youngest didn't quite like it in the end!! LOL

CULLA'S TAVERN BY BRADFORD KISSELL (left): This small, unimposing bar at 2029 Riverside Avenue in Minneapolis was a neighborhood fixture for years, serving 25-cent beers, Hank Williams on the jukebox and an occasional game of Yahtzee with owner Kathleen "Culla" Nordin.

A MOTHER'S LOVE BY DUANE BRIDGEMAN (opposite): There is no equal.

NATIVE PRIDE BY KATHY ANDERSON (above): Taken at the Prairie Island Wacipi (powwow).

ALL MEN ARE CREATED EQUAL, THEN A FEW BECOME FIREMEN.
BY CASSANDRA PARKER (right): Farmington, MN.

HIDDEN BEAUTY
BY CAITLIN O'BRIEN (above left): So we snapped some photos in my garage today. We only got a half an hour of light outside since all my friends were too slow when getting ready. We had to go back to my garage. All I used was my lamp from my room, a white sheet and duct tape to hang it up. It's kind of sad I can't afford the real stuff yet. But hopefully one day. :)

INDIAN BRIDE
BY SAIBAL GHOSH (above right): Indian bride.

BEAUTIFUL COSTUME
BY TOUCHER LEE (left): My beautiful angel.

DISCUSSING THE PLAN
BY KIM C. TAYLOR (far left): My son and his wife walking their pasture land.

FURRY FRIENDS
Pets, farm animals and creatures from the zoo.

SNEEZING TIGER, HIDDEN GIRAFFE BY PATRICK STEWART (above): The Como Park Zoo is grrrreat! The giraffe is very hard to see (he's good at hiding).

ELEPHANT REPOSE BY BRIAN BILLADEAU (left): Taken at the Minnesota Renaissance Festival just after opening and the morning light was glowing! The smaller elephant (pictured) walked in front of the large elephant. I like this one because it takes a moment to realize the subject due to the texture-on-texture, lighting and color. In person, especially on the metallic print, the detail is amazing.

GO TEAM!!!!! BY DARCY SIME (far left): I don't know if they were fans of the Bison or fans of the Pronghorn - but they sure were enthusiastically cheering on their team!

AHHHHH! BY R JORDE (above): A polar bear at the Como Park Zoo.

UNUSUAL FARM FRIEND BY JODI PFLEPSEN (top left): Not your usual farm animal but a welcome addition to our Minnesota hobby farm!

REST BY PATRICK CLANCY (bottom left): Proceed with caution.

NORTHERN SAW WHET OWL BY TIM FEENEY (bottom right): I just happened to be walking by Tamarack Nature Center when someone brought out this owl for some air. What a cutie!

WOLF VALENTINES BY SHANNON KUNKLE (opposite): Male & female wolves at the Minnesota Zoo. Photographed on Valentine's Day 2010.

GYPSY HORSES BY TONI THOMAS (above): Visit to Gypsy Dance Ranch. They stopped and posed for a moment. Beautiful, sweet and friendly!

OPPOSITE:

SWEET CHEEKS BY DEB LEE CARSON (1): She whispers in loving words so kind, into the young girl's sweet, clear mind. Come with me my delightful one, and we shall ride off into the sun!

WINDOW TO THE SOUL BY GINA STOCKER (2): In the steady gaze of the horse shines the eloquence that speaks of love, loyalty, strength and courage. "It is the window that reveals to us how willing is his spirit, how generous his heart."

TUESDAY AT THE WINDOW BY RENÉ ROSENGREN (3): We found our cat on a Tuesday in 1987 when she was approximately two weeks old. We fed her Kitten Replacement Formula from a tiny bottle at the start. She had a long life, leaving us just a few months shy of her 20th birthday in 2007.

TRUE LOVE BY CHARLES HEZSELY (4): "You are a winner to me" — goat and goatherd at The Minnesota State Fair.

SUNSET ON THE FARM BY CHANCE ALBERG (5): Sunset on the farm.

A LITTLE CONFUSED BY DARCY SIME (6): I think BOTH of them are confused!

OL' FASHIONED ALARM CLOCK BY TONY KOLLMAN (7): Shot at the Minnesota Zoo.

THE THREE AMIGOS BY ALISSA BERTHIAUME (8): Curious cows coming to see what I was doing. I was taking photos of the barbed wire at first but then they came over so I got this instead :) Menahga, MN.

FRIENDLY FELINE
BY JENNIFER FALLS (above): A friend's cat named Squash curious about the camera. "An animal's eyes have the power to speak a great language." - Martin Buber

BELLA BY HANS MOURITZEN (left): Our new cat taken with my new zoom lens.

CLYDE BY TRACY WALSH (far left): Clyde is a very great Great Dane! His owner sat down next to him for a quick portrait. Taken the spring after Clyde had surgery.

DOG DAYS #2
BY J ARTHUR ANDERSON (opposite): Coolin' off in the river playing keep away.

SCAPES OF ALL SORTS

Landscapes, waterscapes and other dramatic scenes of Minnesota

DREAMING OF AUTUMN BY RYAN TISCHER (above): The unique sandstone quarries and incredible fall colors within Banning State Park, near Hinckley, make for a beautiful autumn hike. Many of the sandstone buildings in cities throughout the upper Midwest used rock from this area around the turn of the last century. Mother Nature has since reclaimed the area. This image was captured along the Kettle River on a calm autumn afternoon.

FALL REFLECTIONS BY JOHN LAMERE (left): Norberg Lake in Bear Head Lake State Park. Zoomed in a little bit. (3-shot HDR.)

MINNEHAHA FALLS BY RYAN ENGSTROM (far left): Shot on a warm morning in June.

COOL NIGHT AT THE COVE BY JAMIE STRICKLAND (above): This is a 6-shot panorama from Cove Point at Cove Point Lodge. Each individual capture was a minute exposure. Images were captured on October 28, 2012 just before 9 p.m. with temperatures in the mid-teens!

SKY DRAMA BY ARIEL ARIEL (left): Sunset at Lake Calhoun. There is a transition of light I noticed in the boat line which I hope you'll find interesting.

MORNING FOG BY LARRY RISSER (opposite): Morning fog and morning coffee are the best.

A BEAUTIFUL AUTUMN DAY
BY SHERRY NICHOLSON (above left):
Minneopa State Park, near Mankato.

SPRING CLEAN
BY FRED T. MILLER (above middle): The
spring sun shone on Hidden Falls in Big
Woods State Park in Nerstrand.

PASTEL
BY GLENDA MUELLER (above right): I
woke up to fog one Saturday morning
and realized what a great opportunity it
was for photos. I drove around a bit and
finally stopped at the local historical
society where I got this shot.

OBERG MOUNTAIN
BY RYAN TISCHER (right): For just a few
days each autumn the Oberg Mountain
overlook on the Superior Hiking Trail
offers viewers a sea of red and oranges.
I was fortunate to arrive at the exact
peak of color in 2010 and capture this
image under afternoon lighting.

FALL SUNRISE OVER HOMER BY AL MUELLER (above): An autumn sunrise over a foggy Mississippi River at Homer. This is a 3 image HDR rendition.

DODGE COUNTY SUNRISE BY RACHEL CAIN (left): Taken across a field just as the sun was coming up.

WINTER MORNING AT SPLIT ROCK BY RON GUERNSEY (above): Dan Hoffman, a great photo bud, and I went up in search of "full moon" shots at Split Rock. I was not successful at that, but had a great time.

SUPERIOR SUNRISE BY ALYSSA BOLDISCHAR (left): One of my favorite things to do when I'm in Duluth is to watch the sunrise over Lake Superior. It's so relaxing. Get up, grab my camera, tripod and some coffee and do some long exposures. Heaven.

EARTH ON HEAVEN BY JEFF OLSEN (above): A calm night on Horseshoe Lake in Richmond, Minn.

CASCADE RIVER FALLS BY ROBERT MEYERS (left): Cascade River Falls in late fall.

A TIME FORGOTTEN BY RYAN ENGSTROM (below): This appears to be the remnants of an old dock on Lake Superior.

THE FLATS BY NATE LINDSTROM (opposite): I was surprised to find the shoreline in this state, as it's not often you see Lake Superior covered in ice all the way to the horizon. I was tempted to try and set foot on it, but ultimately decided to shoot from a slightly higher vantage point. The scene reminded me of desert flats, but the sub-zero temperature did not.

GOPHER ORDNANCE WORKS BY MICK RICHARDS (above left): These leftover pillars are part of a former munitions plant that made gunpowder for the Armed Forces in World War II.

DAYBREAK BY DONOVAN ISDAHL (above right): The sun rising on a foggy day.

STANDING TALL AMONGST THE OTHER BIRCHES BY H BROWN TON (right): Hiking along a trail and looked up to catch this birch standing tall and brilliant in the sun amongst the others that had already lost their leaves.

HOK SI LA PARK BY SHAWN TURNER (opposite): I stopped here on a whim after a photo shoot in Lake City. Came up with this shot.

PATH THROUGH THE FIELD BY JEFF BARTELT (above): A path wanders through a field of corn in southeastern Minnesota.

HAY BALES BY JELIETA WALINSKI ED.D (left): Amidst the fog are hay bales!

UNIFORM CORN BY BRADFORD KISSELL (opposite): I love how the infrared camera I used emphasized the sun's rays breaking through the clouds and the contrast of the new growth in this field in late spring.

GREENER PASTURES BY JOHN NIEMI (above): Farm fields laid out against the rolling hills of southeastern Minnesota near Harmony.

FARM SCENE BY ADAM JOHNSON (right): A Minnesota farm scene.

WINTER'S LAST STAND BY RYAN TISCHER (far right): Winters can be long and arduous in northern Minnesota, but also beautiful in their own right.

**LITTLE HOUSE ON THE PRAIRIE
BY LISA WILLEY** (left): A capture of an old house I stumbled upon. I was in the Battle Lake area and I wanted to photograph an old schoolhouse. I stopped a police officer to see if he knew where the schoolhouse was. He took me to this instead. I was pleasantly surprised.

**EARLY SUMMER MORNING SUNRISE
BY DAVE HAUGE** (bottom left): Summer morning sunrise just at the right angle for this Minnesota farm shot and if you look closely you can see a jet contrail behind the windmill.

**WINTER FARM
BY CHRISTINA OLSEN** (bottom right): Winter on a farm in Nowthen, Minnesota.

**NESTLED IN THE HOAR FROST
BY RON TRAEGER** (right): Under clear frosty nights, soft ice crystals sometimes form on any object that has been chilled below the freezing point by radiation cooling. This deposit of ice crystals is known as hoar frost. These interlocking ice crystals become one of the most prominent features of a 'winter wonderland' day.

SUNRISE SHADOWS BY BILL WALSH (bottom left): Sunrise shadows.

FOG AND HORSES BY PATRICK CLANCY (bottom right): An amazing fog rolled in as I was packing up after shooting a wedding. I decided to explore the area nearby and happened across this breathtaking scene.

THE HILLS BY DEB LEE CARSON (opposite): A foggy morning view of a farm tucked against the hills in our valley along Wells Creek.

MILKY WAY STARS OVER CORN BY AARON GROEN (above): Milky Way shines brightly over a cornfield next to Hawk's Nest Lake, Ivanhoe, Minn. Single exposure shot with flashlight used to light corn.

TOWERING ECLIPSE BY JIM ERICSON (right): Caught the eclipsed sun as it dipped below the horizon, seemingly between these two TV towers.

BARN BY AARON GROEN (far right): Milky Way shines brightly over this old barn near Luverne, Minn.

SLOW DOWN BY SCOTT CANFIELD (below): In our daily hurry to get things done or get somewhere we miss some of nature's most spectacular displays.

LANDMARK CENTER
BY PATRICK CLANCY (right): Cathedral overlooks Landmark Center. Taken from the Penthouse atop the Lowry Building in downtown. I had to walk out on the ledge...made some people watching in adjacent buildings a bit nervous I think.

FROM THE FOSHAY II
BY MARK NICHOLSON (opposite): Larry and I were in town tonight celebrating a birthday. Main event — shooting from the Foshay Tower. Did you know there are some real nice vents that pump out warm air on the observation deck? A pleasant surprise for us.

WINTER NIGHT IN ST. PAUL
BY JUSTIN BROWN (bottom left): On a cold night in St. Paul, the lights of the city illuminate the sky.

DISTANT NEIGHBORS
BY MATTHEW PRAZAK (bottom right): A gloomy Minneapolis skyline lurks behind the St. Paul Cathedral at the 2013 Redbull Crashed Ice Races.

ST PAUL SUNSET 2 BY NATE GIBSON (above): One of the perks of living on the 29th floor in the beautiful city of St. Paul.

OPPOSITE:

ICONIC BY ALEX FRASER (1): Downtown Minneapolis from the 24th St. pedestrian bridge (the one everyone always shoots from).

INTO THE CITY BY RYAN ENGSTROM (2): Shot at sunset on walkway over 35.

UNTITLED BY BOB ISRAEL (3): Minneapolis, Minn.

12TH & NICOLLET MALL BY DOUG WALLICK (4): The intersection of 12th & Nicollet Mall, with a couple of buses heading towards me, and the steeple of Westminster Church in the foreground.

MISSISSIPPI BLUE BY JAMES GILLILAND (5): The cold of winter and the lights of the 35W bridge turning the mighty Mississippi into a blue mirror.

MILL CITY COLOR PALETTE BY MARK GOODMAN (6): Minneapolis reflects so many different colors on the river. They make a wonderful companion to the Stone Arch Bridge.

NIGHT LIGHTS IN THE CITY BY KATHY LARSON (7): A cold winter's night!

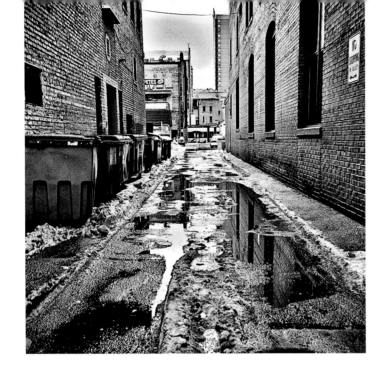

DOWNTOWN PUDDLES BY BETSY GRACA (above left): Melting snow turns to puddles in a downtown alley in January 2013.

MYSTIC WALK BY CURTIS MILLER (above right): One of my favorite places at Springbrook Nature Center in Coon Rapids, MN.

VISION TUNNEL BY RON GUERNSEY (right): This is just under the scenic version of Hwy. 61 along Lake Superior.

UNTITLED
BY ANN GINSBURGH HOFKIN (top left):
View of the 10th Avenue Bridge in
downtown Minneapolis.

PATH INTO GARDEN
BY STEVEN SHOR (top right): Taken
in late fall at Normandale Japanese
Garden.

**SPRING ARRIVES AT THE UNIVERSITY OF
MINNESOTA LANDSCAPE ARBORETUM**
BY MARK MACLENNAN (bottom): Visitors
walking the trail behind the Woodland
Azalea Garden and Hosta Glade at the
University of Minnesota Landscape
Arboretum in the late April evening.

LIVING IN MINNESOTA
Schooling, industry, farming, working and newsworthy events.

BOXCARS BY ANGELA LUNDBERG (above): Railroad yard, northeast Minneapolis.

LAST SALT BY SHAWN BROWN (left): The Tatjana makes her way into the harbor as the last oceangoing vessel of the shipping season.

HARD AT WORK BY ROBERT WELTON (far left): The crew onboard the "Nels J" (Heritage Marine) breaking ice before the "Roger Blough" enters the Duluth Harbor for winter layup. Spent 12 hours onboard the "Helen J" tug in below-zero weather as the two worked to dock the Blough.

EMPIRE BUILDER FLIES THRU MAPLE SPRINGS BY MIKE VANDENBERG (above): Just a bit behind the advertised time, the eastbound Empire Builder flies through one of the trademark curves south of Lake City in Maple Springs, MN. If you have never taken a trip on the Amtrak from St. Paul to Chicago, it is well worth the time...the scenery is just stunning!

DEPARTING TRAINS BY RYAN CHERNIK (right): This overhead bridge in St. Paul offered a great vantage point for changing crews at the CP railroad yard. Tilt-shift effect implemented in post.

FREIGHT TRAIN NEAR LAKE CITY BY PAUL KAMMEN (bottom left): A freight train moves near Lake City on a fall afternoon.

LETTING OFF A LITTLE STEAM BY NANCY RUDESILL (bottom right): Duluth Harbor.

UNTITLED BY JEREMIAH BROWN (top left): Russell Steel.

GRAIN STORAGE BY ROBERT BALL (top middle): BNSF Northtown local and General Mills grain elevators. Both are a vital part of Minnesota's industry, teaming to provide Cheerios to the world.

HULL RUST MOVERS BY JOHN NIEMI (top right): Hull Rust open pit mine, Hibbing, over 50+ years of digging and still operating.

THE SWITCHMAN BY BRADFORD KISSELL (left): Nothing like a railyard at night for a little drama.

BRINGING DOWN THE TREE BY JOHN RICHARDSON (above): A sudden overnight storm damages a backyard tree. It needs to come down before it hits the house.

PRINTING THE LOCAL PAPER BY MERCY NYGAARD (left): The Sauk Rapids Sentinel originated in 1868. It became the Sauk Rapids Herald and is the longest-running newspaper in Minnesota still running today. Pictured here working the intertype is Roland Doroff, the current owner of 42 years.

CONSERVATION CORPS AT WORK BY MICK RICHARDS (opposite top left): These young ladies and men were repairing the stairway at Tettegouche State Park. It washed out in the June 2012 storm. To the far left, you can see the shiny new bolts in the stairs they were working on and had replaced. This is on the far end of the park — for those who've been there, you can imagine the long walk and stairs you have to traverse to get here. This is at the Baptism Falls pool where the falls goes into the river on the far side of the park. They carried all the lumber and tools — you can see they're holding power tools. Yep, they carried in one of those 50 pound generators. These kids really worked hard. They asked if I would be interested in carrying their generator out but I begged off with the excuse of having a camera backpack and a heavy tripod. Excellent job done, CC!

IDLE, BUT NOT FORGOTTEN BY DREW SANDBERG (opposite bottom left): Pragmatic and beautiful, if not dangerous.

PAGAMI FIRE FIGHTER BY KEN HUPILA (opposite right): One of over 800 firefighters on last fall's Pagami Creek Fire.

FROM PULP TO PAPER BY PAUL KRUMREI (above): Piles of wood at Blandin Paper Company waiting to be made into paper.

BALANCING ACT BY DAN ROGNESS (left): A roofer working for D.R. Horton on a house under construction in Prior Lake.

THROW ANOTHER LOG ON THE FIRE BY KEN GRESHOWAK (far left): A little extra fuel required during a long week of subzero weather.

A DAY IN THE LIFE
BY MICHAEL AGUIRRE (right): The things we take for granted are suddenly quite aware on our simple trip to the store, for necessities or just the daily grind - the job!

TRANSPORTATION - MINNESOTA STYLE
BY SALLY HAWKINS (bottom left): This team picked out their Christmas tree and, I imagine, were heading back home. The longer sled rope broke halfway through the intersection, but once across the street the repair was made and they were comfortably on their way again.

SNOWPLOWS AT WORK
BY ROSE SHEA (bottom right): Hurray for the plows! Without them life wouldn't be so easy in the winter in Minnesota.

MASTER CANOE BUILDERS AT WORK.
BY GEORGE PETERS (opposite): What could be more Minnesotan than building canoes for Boundary Waters trips. Northwest Canoe, St. Paul.

FARM BOAT
BY JELIETA WALINSKI ED.D (left):
Unique boat on the farm.

THE OLD BARN
BY MARY CARLSON (bottom left): Taken
just before sunset when the light was
great.

BARN IN THE ROUND
BY RUSSELL LOFGREN JR (bottom right):
Try and find a corner in this old barn....

THE END OF AUGUST IN MINNESOTA
BY JOE ESLER (opposite): Taken just
outside of Hastings.

A RURAL WINTER BY DOUG WALLICK (right): A nice weathered barn on some rolling hills in Loretto.

THE OLD BARN BY JOHN KROHN (bottom left): Old barn marking the site of a long-gone farmstead, near Morgan.

TRACTOR BY MICHAEL SEMAAN (bottom right): Old tractor.

SUGARDALE SUNRISE BY JOHN STOCKER (opposite): Another photograph of this iconic barn. Taken at sunrise.

AN EDUCATION IN STRAWBERRIES BY GRETCHEN ALMS (above): Picking strawberries is always a fun pastime, even if more of the berries end up in our mouths than in the pail. Here a mushy, rotten strawberry sidetracks and disappoints our newest helper.

END OF HARVEST BY FRED T. MILLER (right): The tractor sat silent as another harvest came to an end.

HARVEST'S HAND BY GRETCHEN ALMS (far right): Drier than usual corn yields and decades of farming hasn't diminished this farmer's love for working the land.

TOMATO GIRL BY STEVE SCHNEIDER (top): There is a small window of time when the rising sun gets above the surrounding buildings and gets under the roof at the St. Paul Farmer's Market. For a few minutes it is very sweet light! I loved the light and the young woman with her tomatoes.

QUIET REFLECTION BY GINA STOCKER (bottom left): Reflecting on the past.

JUST NEEDS A NEW COAT OF PAINT BY BRYAN FLANAGAN (bottom right): A nice old relic in Delano, MN.

OPPOSITE:

MOON HARVEST BY DAVID LUNDQUIST (1): An October corn harvest was replete with a full moon rising in the east.

THE DAIRY DEPARTMENT BY JOE ESLER (2): I was looking for some more barns to shoot when I came across this family of cows in front of a red barn. I certainly got all of their attention!

A FARMER'S WORKING LUNCH BY GRETCHEN ALMS (3): Three generations of farmers take a quick break from soybean harvest for a quick picnic lunch in the field for hot dogs, salads and bars.

MAKING HAY BY DENNY LEHMAN (4): A neighbor making hay the old-fashioned way.

SOYBEAN BY DAVE HAUGE (5): This was an early morning summer shot of a Minnesota soybean field and just a few minutes later the sun was behind the clouds.

TOO DRY FOR DINNER BY RICHARD SMITH (6): You would usually find these gulls behind the tractor, snacking on fresh plowed worms and other bugs. Unfortunately, the lack of rain accompanied by the excessive heat this summer left them hungry. I seized this rare opportunity and grabbed a quick picture out of my truck window.

THERESIA GETS AGRICULTURE BY DAVID LUNDQUIST (7): Theresia farms in extreme northwest Minnesota with her husband Keith.

FRIDAY NIGHT LIGHTS
BY CARL SCHULZETENBERG (left): A high school junior waits to enter the game. Who could have guessed at the time, that just a couple years later, he would die in a military helicopter crash. (Image scanned from a negative.)

CHOIR BOYS BY JOHN STOCKER (far left): Taken as the ninth graders were about to begin their first song during a high school choir concert.

G IS FOR GEOGRAPHY
BY STAN WALDHAUSER (following left): Montessori students.

A TIME TO LISTEN
BY STEVE SCHNEIDER (following right): For CURA (Center for Urban and Regional Affairs), I was asked to shoot at Como Park Elementary School for an article on improving education in Minnesota. I found this group assembled in the library, not so very different from the reading time I remember 50+ years ago. That was comforting to me; it was real human-to-human contact... not some solitary child by the glow of an LED screen on some electronic device.

BACK TO SCHOOL BY ANTHONY HANSON (above): I went for a walk, and saw the museum was open with free summer admission. So I called my wife and asked her if she wanted to see it. She did and we went through it, Pope County Museum.

SUMMER FIELD TRIP BY MARK CAVANAUGH (left): A trip to a water park explains both the wet hair and the smile.

HEADED FOR COLLEGE BY JENNIFER WEINER (far left): 2012 Chanhassen High School graduates spending one of their last evenings of summer together before heading off to school!

GRADUATES BY MATT BARBER (below): Southwest H.S. class of 2011 at the Minneapolis Convention Center. Got lucky with a long telephoto shot.

MY FAVORITE COFFEE SHOP BY R JORDE (above left): It was one of those mornings where one could face the day only after warming oneself with a good cup of steaming hot coffee.

DAILY CROSSINGS BY TOMMY SAR (above right top): Lunch rush in downtown Minneapolis.

LATE FALL CLEANING BY DAN ROGNESS (above right bottom): A commercial window washer on the outside of Prior Lake City Hall.

HONORING THE ULTIMATE SACRIFICE BY JIM NOON (right): Harry Bedard, WWII aviator.

THE ELEGANCE OF SIMPLICITY BY THOMAS EICKHOFF (above): No more words needed.

COMING IN FOR A LANDING BY KATHY WELLUMSON (left): Above Lake Nokomis at sunset.

VIKINGS STADIUM BILL BY TOM OLMSCHEID (above): Members of the Vikings World Order rally in the Capitol rotunda for the House and Senate to pass a football stadium bill for the Minnesota Vikings. The House passed the Vikings stadium bill 73-58.

MINNEAPOLIS ARTIST BY TYLER BERGE (right): An artist painting on the Stone Arch Bridge.

10:59 COMES AND GOES BY MICHAEL BENHAM (far right): I went out for a roaming evening shoot with my new fisheye lens (a Samyang 8mm). This was my fourth stop. This is the lightrail station stop for Cedar-Riverside. I started off on the east end of the platform then moved here further in. This is a composite image of two exposures. The left side is the scheduled 10:59 southbound train, and a couple minutes later, the 10:59 northbound train on the right side of the image.

NATURE

The beautiful wildlife, stunning nature and dramatic weather of Minnesota.

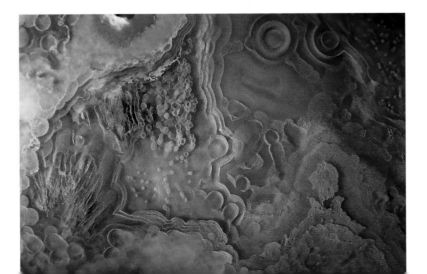

LOVE WINTER BY DEB LEE CARSON (above): "Let us love winter, for it is the spring of genius." - Pietro Aretino. My favorite season, winter in Minnesota! Especially during an incredibly beautiful snowfall!

INTRICATE AGATE BY TIM FEENEY (left): One of my favorite hobbies is to collect Lake Superior agates in the summer, polish them and make macro photos during the winter.

MAGNIFICENT MINNESOTA MAMMATUS BY SUSAN DAHLEN (far left): These clouds were even more stunning than what my lens could capture.

JUMP START BY FRANCO COLAIANNI (above): Lightning strike early May 2012. Did not actually hit the windmill; only a burst in the sky behind it.

STORMY BY ANTHONY HANSON (right): Stormy clouds in the country with swirling clouds above...yay! A storm that moved through in May of 2011 that dropped a lot of hail.

STORM BIRTH BY DREW KOENIG (below): Minnesota storm birth.

OUT FOR A WALK BY RAY KLEMPKA (opposite): It was the first big storm of the season. It was a perfect time to be out in the cool, crisp air, white landscapes and for making tracks in the snow. It was a moment that needed to be shared with your closest of friends. It was time to go out for a walk.

FORGOTTEN BY CHERI BRANDT (above): One lone clothespin left on the line. Scanned from a film original.

WINTER IS JUST AROUND THE CORNER... BY REBECCA SMITH (right above): Frosty leaves in the morning...

FORGET ME NOTS BY LISA PALMER FLEMING (right bottom): Unforgettable little patch on the Baptism River near Finland.

PANE PAINTING BY EILEEN SABES (above): A window can be many things, such as a way to look out at nature or a way to look within it.

TRANQUILITY BY BONNIE J. HAGELBERGER (left): Ground cover adds to the sense of peace and tranquility one experiences while strolling through Noerenberg Gardens on the shore of Lake Minnetonka.

THE END OF FALL BY MEL PEIFER (below): Before the last leaves fell...

BUSY BEE - EMPLOYEE OF THE YEAR!
BY LARRY KAASA (top left): If making honey can be considered an industry in Minnesota, then this bee should be Employee of the Year for all the pollen she has collected!

SURF'S UP! BY PRIYA SAIHGAL (top right): Fly riding the iris petal wave at the Como Conservatory. I think the little guy got too much water in its system. :P

EASTERN TAILED-BLUE BUTTERFLY
BY MARK ANDERSEN (bottom): Eastern Tailed-blue Butterflies feed on various legumes and are known to secrete a substance which is favored by some ant species. The ant in turn protects the larva of the butterfly from other predators.

OPPOSITE:

RED-TAILED HAWK FALL FLAVOR BY MIKE LENTZ (1): Red-tailed Hawk fall flavor.

SWANS TAKEOFF BY NADAV CASSUTO (2): I waited for an hour on the ice for the swans to takeoff (at sunset).

GROUNDED SNOWY OWL BY TERRY CRAYNE (3): Does he really think he's sneaking up on me?

READY TO COURT BY NADAV CASSUTO (4): The next step was to stick its tongue out. :-)

ATTITUDE! BY LARRY KAASA (5): Green Heron - Tamarack Nature Center.

BABY WOOD DUCK JUMPER BY MIKE LENTZ (6): Baby Wood Duck leaving a natural nest cavity.

BABY BLUE BY TOM SAMUELSON (7): Bluebirds are some of my favorite subjects and when this baby, who was just learning to fly, stopped by I had to capture this image.

FEEDING AT THE RIVER BY AL MUELLER (8): A Bald Eagle gliding over the Mississippi River looking for a fish to grab.

BEAR CUB WATCHING BY LOUIS HADDAD (above): Cute little guy.

TOWERING PINE TREES BY BONNIE FECHTER (right): Love how the trees are "standing" in the straight lines....

WINTER FLOW BY L. E. SWANSON (opposite): Kettle River.

MUSICAL BIRDS BY MEL PEIFER (following): Shooting from the bridge, going over the Coon Rapids Dam, gives me a bird's eye view of the birds.

THE MIST BY SHELLY ANGELL-GRAVGAARD (below): The Playground.

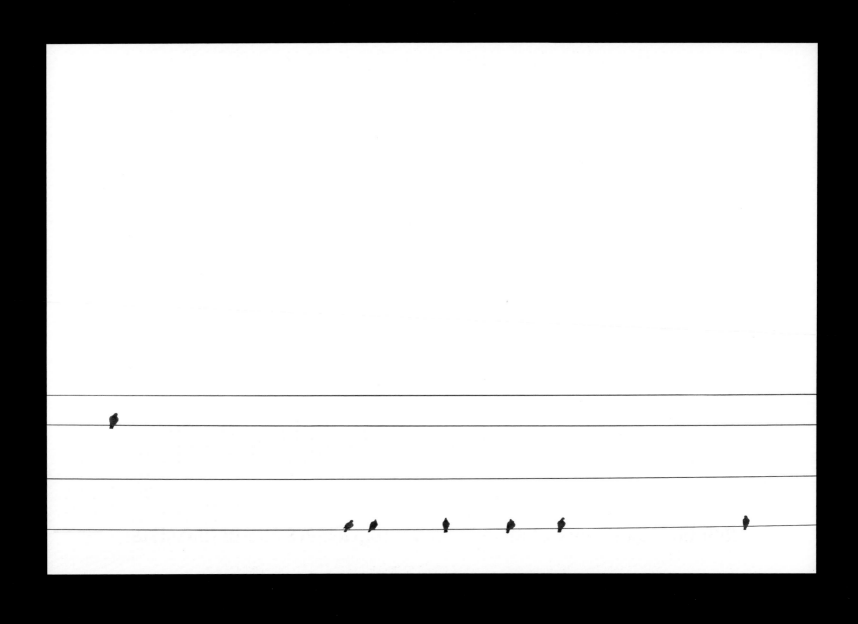

Help Find the Best of Minnesota

Join the community of Minnesota photographers and enthusiasts!

Vote to find the best of Minnesota, order prints or upload your own take on Minnesota at:

captureminnesota.com

Community Stats

The Capture Minnesota II book was created by the efforts of Minnesota folks who have a passion for their local community and an eye for great photography. The community of users at Capture Minnesota (captureminnesota.com) has spent countless hours shaping this book with submissions, votes and comments. Its their editing power that determined which photos deserved publication in this book and which photos our editors had to consider for publication. Along the way, users generated some astounding statistics (below) in terms of activity on the Capture Minnesota web site. Our sincere thanks to every user who dedicated their time to shaping the Capture Minnesota II book.

222,705
photos

6,898
photographers

8,786,491
votes

798,981
comments

25,288
users

900,204
loves

Community Leaders

The active online community of users at Capture Minnesota (captureminnesota.com) shaped this book with its submissions, votes, comments, etc. Below you'll find the community leaders in each of six categories: top voter, the user with the most votes cast; top promoter, the user who promoted the contest via email the most; most followed, the user whom other users followed most; top commenter, the user who commented on photos the most; most decorated, the user with the most photo awards; and most dug, the user with the most "dig it" votes across all photos.

1. Top voter
Dorothy Kvittum
204,065 votes cast

2. Top promoter
Jack Hedberg
310 shares

3. Most followed
Jelieta Walinski Ed.D
1,052 followers

4. Top commenter
Alice McKinney
29,492 comments

5. Most decorated
Eileen Sabes
399 photo awards

6. Most Dug
John Heino
62,753 dig it votes

Winners

When picking from 222,705 photos, it's difficult to nail down what separates the best from the rest — especially when so many photos are so good. To help, we enlisted thousands of local folks to vote for their favorite shots. The response was epic: 8,786,491 votes were cast. The voting helped shape what would eventually be published in this book. Along the way, the votes produced the grand-prize and cover winners below.

Grand-prize winner
Photo by Max Haynes
Page 24

Cover winner
Photo by Mark Goodman
Cover, page 99

Runners-up
These photos finished just behind the grand-prize photo in total score.

Photo Credits: Beau Liddell, Barb Determan, Troy Hattemer, Toni Kahnke

Thank You

We at *tpt* have enjoyed another great year working on Capture Minnesota! And we're so grateful to everyone who has shared their wonderful images with this community of talented photographers. Minnesota is a special place and we trust that this book we have created together captures the beauty of our state in a remarkable way.

We'd like to thank Medica for its generous financial support of this project. Without it, this book simply would not be possible.

Finally, we'd like to publicly acknowledge all of our members who support *tpt* with their donations.

tpt   MEDICA®